Tomorrow's World

TRANSPORT IN THE FUTURE

Mark Lambert

Wayland

Tomorrow's World

First published in 1986 by Wayland (Publishers) Limited
61 Western Road, Hove, East Sussex BN3 1JD, England

British Library Cataloguing-In-Publication Data
Lambert, Mark
Transport in the Future – (Tomorrow's World)
Wayland (Publishers)
1. Transportation – Juvenile Literature
I. Title II. Series
380.5 HE152

ISBN 0–85078–712–2

Phototypeset by Kalligraphics Ltd., Redhill, Surrey
Printed in Italy by G. Canale & C.S.p.A., Turin
Bound in Great Britain at The Bath Press, Avon

Contents

Moving people

Transport is the business of moving people and goods from one place to another. Ideally, this is done quickly and efficiently, using the least possible amount of fuel. The designers of future city transport systems will have a number of problems to overcome. Cities will probably be much larger than they are today and many more people will be needing transport. In addition, the available fuels are likely to be very expensive, so efficiency and economy will become all-important.

In the vast cities of the future, good public transport systems will be essential.

Many people depend on trains to take them to and from work.

City transport

One major problem of city transport is that the 'flow' of people is not even. Huge numbers of people need transport during the morning 'rush hours', but in between these periods far fewer people are travelling. So, above all, a city transport system must be flexible. It must cope with large numbers of passengers trying to reach a wide range of destinations during peak periods, and provide a more restricted, economical service at off-peak times.

In the future, as now, those who live and work in a city will be able to choose from several different types of transport. An underground railway system will link key points in the city. Above ground there will be buses, taxis and possibly even moving walkways to carry people to specific destinations. But instead of operating independently, all these means of transport will link up with one another, forming an integrated transport system. Private cars will probably not be allowed on the streets, and traffic congestion should become a thing of the past.

Underground trains provide an efficient transport service within big cities.

Inner-city trains

Modern underground systems use multiple-unit electric trains, in which each coach, or unit, is powered by its own electric motors. Electric current is collected from a third 'live' rail, either in between or beside the two carrying rails. In the foreseeable future, electric trains are unlikely to be replaced in underground systems – they are fast and do not produce fumes.

However, electric trains are not cheap to run and the designers of future underground systems will be trying to reduce the power needed to propel trains along. A considerable power-saving could be achieved by reducing the friction between the wheels and the rails. Maglev (magnetic levitation) trains could eliminate this form of friction by using magnetism to lift the coaches of the train off the tracks, doing away with wheels completely (see page 22).

Friction also occurs between the surface of a train and the air. In an underground tunnel, air becomes a considerable barrier that a train has to push out of the way. One solution to this problem would be to remove the air in the tunnel, thus creating a vacuum. A maglev train running in a vacuum tunnel would be totally frictionless and over long distances could achieve very high speeds. Passengers would enter and leave such a train by means of sealed airlocks. Vacuum underground trains will not be cheap to operate and maintain, but if electricity costs soar, they could become economic.

This American people mover cabin operates along an overhead track.

People movers

People movers are small, tracked cabins, designed to carry passengers quickly from one busy place to another. In cities, people movers could be used between major car parks, railway stations and airport terminals. One design foresees people mover cabins travelling along special tracks in streets, through buildings and even up and down the sides of buildings like lifts. The cabins would be hailed electronically by passengers at special pick-up points.

An eighty-passenger people mover in use at Gatwick Airport, England.

Autotaxis

A city of the future may well be equipped with a system of autotaxis. These will be particularly useful for tourists and people entering the city by road. Visitors will park their own cars outside the city limits and then walk a short distance to the nearest 'call-up' point. A press of a button will summon the nearest empty autotaxi. Once inside, the travellers will use the autotaxi's computer to help them decide where they want to go. The autotaxi will then carry them to their destination, finding its way by following cables buried in the roadway and coded radio signals from 'bleepers' at the side of the road. Microwave radar will help the autotaxi detect the position and speed of other vehicles and pedestrians.

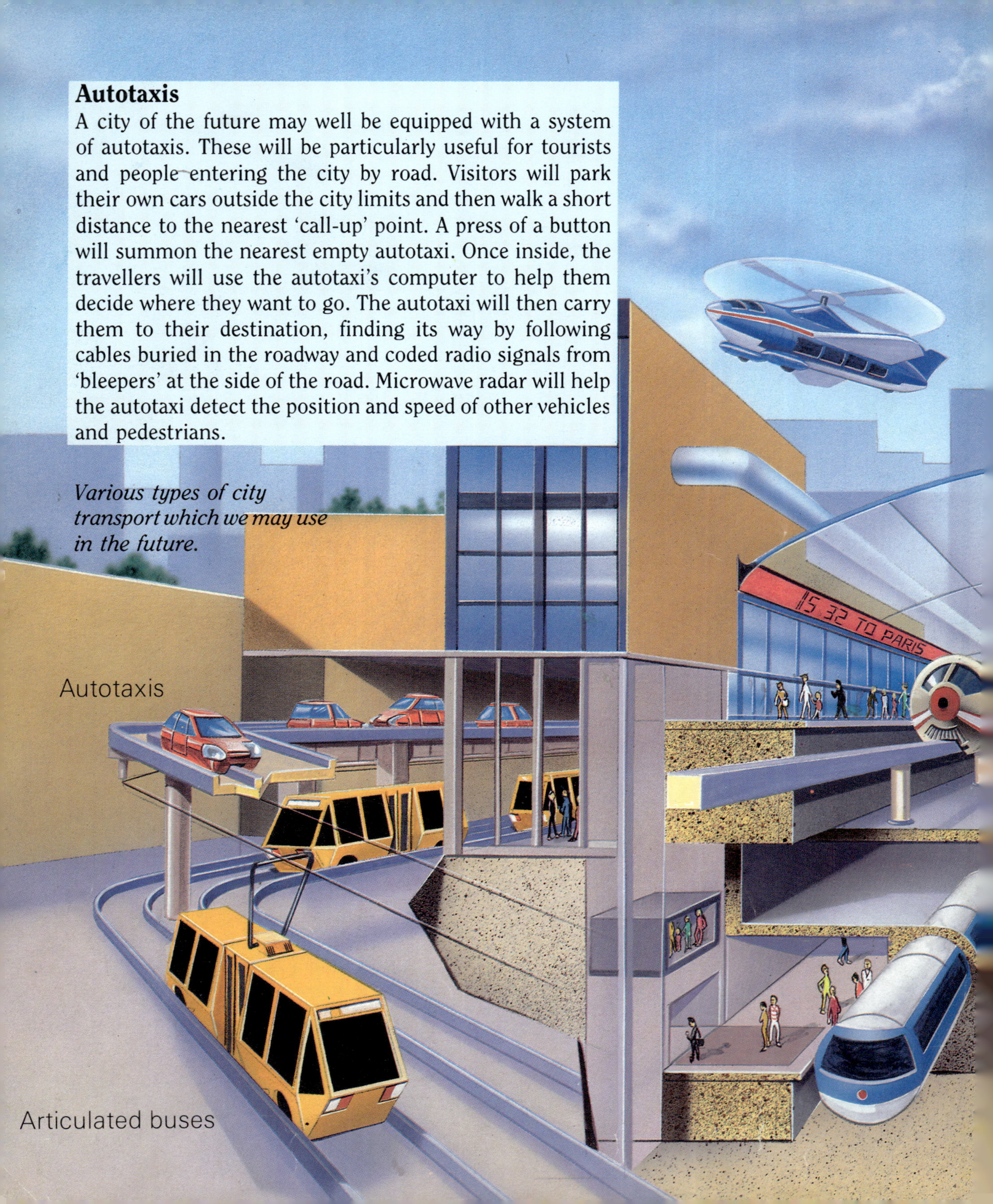

Various types of city transport which we may use in the future.

City buses

Buses hold more people than taxis and will be an essential feature of future city transport, particularly in suburban areas where underground train systems are uneconomic to build. Future buses will probably be articulated, automatic or semi-automatic vehicles. On the most commonly-used routes they will be powered by electricity from overhead cables, but they could also be operated on other routes, using battery power or diesel engines.

Future buses may, like autotaxis, be guided to pick-up platforms by following loops of cable set in the road. Others may have their own concrete trackways and use small, horizontal guide-wheels to keep them in the tracks. Such tracks could be laid alongside ordinary roadways, constructed as overhead trackways, or even laid in underground tunnels.

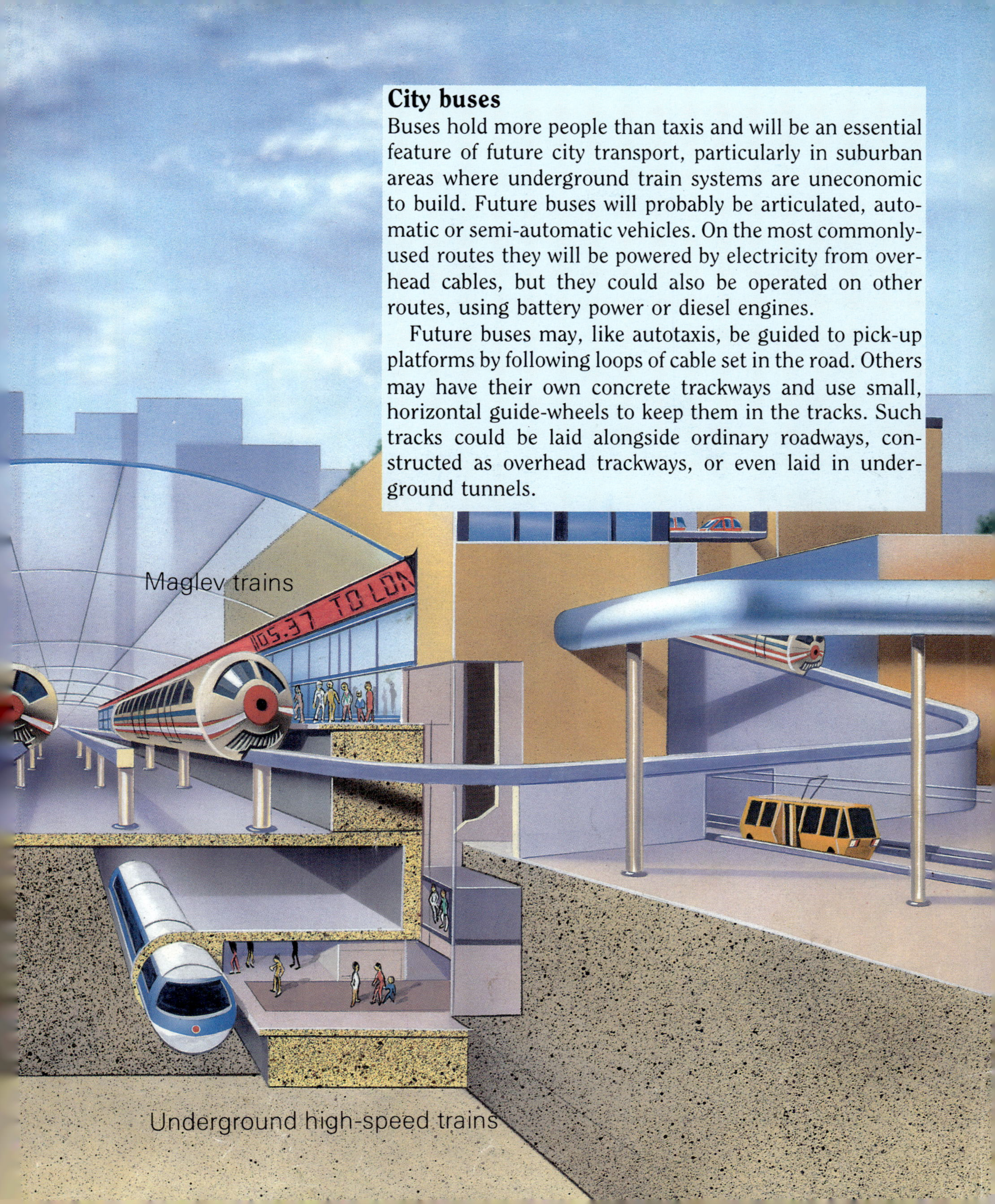

Future cars

As the cost of extracting and refining oil increases and the world's reserves dwindle, petrol and diesel fuel will become more and more expensive. And any fuels that replace them are not likely to be cheap. So, above all, cars of the future will have to be very economic in their fuel consumption. In addition they will have to be safe, comfortable and non-polluting.

Streamlining

A good deal of the energy required to accelerate a car and maintain its speed is used in overcoming air resistance, or drag. This is caused in several ways. Firstly, there is the resistance of the mass of air in front of the car. Secondly, as the air rushes over the car's surface, friction tends to slow the car down. Lastly, as the air leaves the rear of the car, whirlpools of moving air are created and these, too, tend to pull the car back.

As now, future cars will be very streamlined: today's Renault Alpine V6 racing model (left), and a future concept car designed by Lotus (above).

Car designers test models of their proposed cars in wind tunnels. Every design is studied to see how air flows over each curve and angle, including underneath the car. The aim is to reduce the drag on the car to as low a level as possible. But in searching for the ideal streamlined shape of car, designers have to consider other factors as well: there has to be enough space for the mechanical components, the passengers and their luggage; the car must also handle well under all conditions; it must be possible to mass-produce the car at a reasonable price, and its appearance must appeal to the buying public.

Reducing pollution

One of the major problems of modern cars is that they emit polluting chemicals from their exhausts. During the 1920s, petrol manufacturers began adding a chemical compound to petrol to prevent 'knocking' (unintended, damaging explosions in the engine). However, this chemical contains the poisonous substance lead, which is expelled from the exhaust. In Britain in the early 1980s, 7,000 tonnes of lead were being emitted into the atmosphere each year!

Today, in a number of countries, lead in petrol is either banned or is being reduced. Many modern cars can now run on lead-free petrol and it is to be hoped that toxic car fumes will soon become a thing of the past.

Coldwell Banker
Coldwell Banker
4th St
EXIT 1/4 MI
6th St
55

Until all cars run on lead-free petrol, heavy traffic will continue to pollute the air.

Other polluting chemicals emitted from car exhausts include nitrogen oxides and the highly-poisonous gas, carbon monoxide. In addition, some unburned petrol chemicals, or hydrocarbons, are emitted and these are acted upon by sunlight to create chemicals that can form smog under some conditions. In America and Japan, there are now laws designed to reduce the amounts of these polluting chemicals. In these countries, cars have a device called a three-way catalytic converter. This is situated in the exhaust system and removes pollutants from the exhaust gases. In addition, car manufacturers are now working on special 'lean-burn' engines, in which the air/fuel ratio is greater. This lowers the temperature at which the fuel burns and reduces the amount of nitrogen oxides produced.

Lean-burn engines have the advantage that they consume less fuel. In the near future, all new cars in Europe may be fitted with lean-burn engines, together with simple devices for removing carbon monoxide.

New fuels for cars

A number of different fuels are being considered as replacements for petrol. In Brazil, cars run on gasohol, a mixture of ethyl alcohol and petrol. The ethyl alcohol, or ethanol, is made by fermenting sugar, produced from sugar cane. Researchers are now looking for ways of producing other fuels cheaply, and it is now possible to make high-grade fuel from all kinds of plants, including those that grow on scrubland. This means that food-producing land does not necessarily have to be used for fuel plants.

In the Philippines, some vehicles have been converted to run on producer gas. This is made by burning wood or charcoal in a device called a gasifier, and it contains up to 15 per cent hydrogen.

Pure hydrogen is also suitable for use in cars, but is difficult to handle. As a gas it is highly flammable and takes up a lot of space. As a liquid it must be kept at a temperature of below −253°C (−423°F). The first experimental hydrogen-powered car was developed in 1980 by DFVLR, the West German aerospace research organization.

This Brazilian attendant is filling up a car with ethanol, an alternative fuel.

The fuel tank of this converted BMW car was a highly-insulated flask containing liquid hydrogen.

Alternatively, hydrogen may be kept in a tank containing grains of a metal alloy which can readily absorb the hydrogen, forming a metal hydride. When this is heated, hydrogen is given off. However, a metal hydride tank will be heavy (which will increase fuel consumption), and refilling will be a slow process. Whilst at present there is no cheap way of mass-producing hydrogen, it is considered by many people to be the 'fuel of the future'. Certainly, if hydrogen can be used, cars will become pollution-free.

Gas turbines, electric cars and hybrids

A gas turbine engine, like a piston engine, uses fuel derived from oil. But there is no reason why gas turbines should not be made to run on other fuels instead. A gas turbine has several advantages over a piston engine. It rotates instead of moving to and fro, and therefore runs more smoothly, needing only a simple gearbox and transmission in order to drive the wheels of a car. Improvements in the acceleration of gas turbine engines have recently been made, and they may soon appear in production cars.

An alternative to cars with internal combustion engines are electric cars, which have existed for over eighty years. However, a modern electric car has various disadvantages. Several heavy and bulky batteries are needed to power the motor, but these wear out quickly and are expensive to replace. In addition, both the range and speed of an electric car are too low to be acceptable to modern drivers.

At present, hybrid cars show more promise for the future than electric cars. A hybrid car has a diesel engine, but instead of driving the wheels directly, it drives a generator which charges a battery. This supplies current to electric motors, which drive the wheels. The advantage of this arrangement is that all the starting, stopping, accelerating and decelerating is done by the electric motors. The diesel engine runs at a constant speed and the car therefore uses less fuel than a conventional diesel-engined car.

This economical electric car runs on a rechargable battery and causes no pollution.

Seat belts can prevent passengers from being badly injured in an accident.

Safer cars for tomorrow

Safety is becoming increasingly important in new car designs. The basis of a safe car is a passenger compartment surrounded by a rigid 'cage' and strengthened doors. The engine and luggage compartments are designed to crumple on impact and bumpers are mounted on shock absorbers.

In a crash, the engine is pushed under the passenger 'cage', and most of the energy from the car's momentum is absorbed by the vehicle rather than by the people inside. A special soft 'skin' at the front of the car helps protect pedestrians from injury in low-speed collisions.

Other safety features include seat belts and collapsable steering wheels, which are continually being improved. However, the fact remains that, in the hands of a human driver, a car is a potentially lethal machine.

One solution to this problem may be to replace the human driver with a computer. At present there are cars with computers that control the ignition timing, fuel supply and braking. In the near future, other systems, such as suspension and gears, will come under computer control. One day perhaps all the systems of a car will be fully automatic. Microwave radar will prevent collisions, and laser devices will monitor road conditions so that cars are driven safely at all times.

This diagram shows how the rigid zone of a car resists impact in a collision.

External view of car involved in a collision

Cross-sectional view of car involved in a collision

Tomorrow's trains

During the 1850s steam trains on the Great Western Railway took several hours to travel the 179 kilometres (112 miles) between London and Bristol. In 1984 a modern HST (High Speed Train) completed the journey in less than one hour. Speed is important in today's railway systems and this is reflected reflected in the design of modern trains.

In the days of steam, a train consisted of a heavy locomotive which pulled a collection of coaches. In contrast, a modern locomotive is an integral part of the train it is pulling. Therefore the whole train is a more streamlined shape. In multiple unit trains there is no distinct locomotive; each coach is driven by its own electric motors.

British Rail's high-speed 125 train and a model of its successor, the Electra (inset).

A bullet-nosed Hikari train passing Mount Fuji in Japan.

Examples of this type of train can be found in many parts of the world. British HSTs can reach speeds of 200 km/h (125 mph), and in 1981 the British APT (Advanced Passenger Train) achieved a speed of 261 km/h (163 mph). Unfortunately this train has not fulfilled early expectations – the much publicized tilting mechanism has never really worked properly. Its successor will be a lightweight, streamlined train called the Electra. This will have a top speed of 225 km/h (141 mph), and should be in use in the early 1990s.

The world's fastest train is the French TGV *(Train à Grande Vitesse)*, which has a top speed of 270 km/h (169 mph). In Japan the bullet-nosed Hikari ('lightning') trains, which run on the Shinkansen line between Tokyo and Osaka, regularly reach speeds of 210 km/h (131 mph) on their specially-designed track.

Power for trains

Most of today's fastest trains are electrically powered, using electricity supplied from overhead cables. Electric traction has several advantages. It is clean, acceleration is rapid, and hill climbing is much easier. So in the near future electric trains are likely to remain the most popular. Where electrification of railways is too expensive or impractical, diesel-electric trains can be used.

Steam power, much cheaper than electricity or diesel fuel, is generally thought of as a relic of a bygone age. However, engineers are currently developing a new type of steam locomotive which bears little resemblance to the

The French Train à Grande Vitesse *achieves the highest speeds in the world.*

smoke-belching locomotives of the early 1900s. As with former steam locomotives, the fuel for the new engine is coal. But no human stoker is needed; the coal is automatically fed into the boiler, and burned in a specially-designed combustion chamber at a relatively low temperature 1,000°C (1,832°F). No smoke or ash is left to escape into the air and no polluting gases are produced.

Heat from the firebox is used to produce steam in a boiler. Like the older steam locomotive, this is used to drive the wheels by means of pistons attached to cranks. But the exhaust steam does not escape through the chimney; instead it is condensed, cooled and re-used.

Trains without wheels

Metal wheels on metal tracks are noisy and both wheels and track tend to wear away. One way of reducing this problem is to use longer-lasting rubber tyres – as fitted on the new metro in Lille, France. Another system uses magnetic levitation (maglev) to lift a train off the track. This has the added advantage that much greater speeds can be reached. In December 1979, an experimental Japanese maglev train achieved 517 km/h (322 mph).

Magnetic levitation is based on the fact that like magnetic poles repel each other, and unlike poles attract each other. Two main systems are currently being researched. One, known as electrodynamic suspension (EDS) uses permanent magnets on the train and a series of coils on the track. As the train moves along, the magnets on the train create magnetic fields in the coils, which repel the train magnets. The main problem with the EDS system is that the powerful train magnets have to be kept at a very low temperature by surrounding them with liquid helium at −269°C (−452°F). So engineers are now concentrating on a different maglev system known as electromagnetic suspension (EMS).

A magnetic field keeps this Japanese Maglev railcar 'floating' in the air.

In an EMS system, the track contains permanent magnets which face downwards. Electromagnets are suspended beneath the train so that they face upwards towards the track magnets. When the electromagnets are energized, they are attracted upwards towards the track magnets. A disadvantage is that, unlike the EDS system, the EMS system needs very fine computer control. At present, engineers are still working on the microprocessors and programs needed to achieve this.

Maglev railcars in use near Birmingham Airport, England.

Maglev trains will be propelled by a type of electromagnetic motor called a linear induction motor. The main drawbacks of maglev trains are likely to be their cost and the difficulty of creating suitable point systems for transferring trains from one track to another. So although they will be capable of great speeds, it is more likely that they will be used for moving people around large cities.

Today, computers are widely used to co-ordinate railway networks.

Another possible future railway is the atmospheric or pneumatic railway. This idea was first devised by Isambard Kingdom Brunel, the great railway engineer. Brunel's atmospheric train was attached to a piston which fitted tightly into a cast iron pipe. A stationary steam engine pumped air out of the pipe ahead of the piston and air pressure behind the piston forced it along the pipe, moving the train with it. A stretch of this railway was built between Exeter and Newton Abbot in Devon, England. But it was soon abandoned because of the difficulty in ensuring a good, airtight seal in the pipe. However, using modern materials and techniques, it should be possible to build such a railway.

A different version of the atmospheric railway has been suggested in America. Instead of just a piston being enclosed in a pipe, the whole train could be enclosed in a sealed tunnel deep underground. Air would be pumped out of the tunnel ahead of the train, which would therefore be pushed along by atmospheric pressure. Speeds of up to 800 km/h (500 mph) could be achieved theoretically in this type of railway.

Automatic railways

Automation is already appearing in our railway systems. Signals, points and track circuits (which indicate the locations of trains) can all be controlled by computer. The French metro networks of Paris and Lille now operate computer-controlled trains, and in fact the Lille metro has not used drivers since 1983. In Japan also there is a 10 kilometre (6 mile) line in Kobe that has operated driver-less trains since 1984. As computer technology improves and the mechanical devices needed to control trains become more reliable, more and more of the world's railways will become automatic.

The driverless trains of the Lille metro in France are operated from a computerized control room.

On and under the sea

Nearly three-quarters of the Earth's surface is covered by ocean, so sea transport will always be needed. Ships will never be as fast as aeroplanes, but a large ship can carry a great deal more than the largest aircraft – and at considerably less cost.

In the future, therefore, larger and larger transport ships may appear. Such ships will probably be built in huge floating dry docks and, once afloat, will never enter a port. Instead, they will be loaded and unloaded several kilometres offshore. This will be done very quickly, using the LASH (lighter aboard ship) system. Lighters (barges) loaded with goods will be towed out to the transport ships and taken on board. The ship may be lowered into the water, allowing the lighters to float on. At the other end of the journey, the lighters will be off-loaded into the water again and towed into port.

Ships without sailors

Using satellite navigation equipment, it is now possible to pinpoint the position of a ship very accurately. By 1990 the Navstar system will consist of eighteen satellites orbiting the Earth. By locking on to the signals from any four of these satellites, a navigator anywhere in the world will be able to fix his ship's position to within a few metres.

Eventually, as a ship's equipment becomes fully automated, there will be no need for a crew on board at all. Instead, satellite systems will be used to navigate the ship from a shore-based station. An on-board computer will receive the incoming signals and be able to direct the ship from port to port, avoiding collisions with other ships and steering clear of bad weather.

Special ships

As now, there will be specialized ships in the future. There may be sail-assisted cruise liners for those travellers who like to see the world in a leisurely fashion. Container ships,

The LASH system is an effective way of loading goods onto a huge ship.

Above *A hydrofoil can travel much faster than conventional ships.*

bulk tankers, ferries, hovercraft, lifeboats and navel vessels will all still be needed. Among the smaller vessels will be hydrofoils for high speed work. The foils of such boats act like underwater wings to lift the hull out of the water and thus reduce water-resistance.

Power for ships

Early steamships were fuelled by coal. Today, with the price of coal at about one-third of the price of bunker oil, coal-fired ships seem set to make a comeback. One British company, Macawber Engineering Ltd, has devised a system for feeding powdered coal along pipes, using air pressure. The coal is stored in large bunkers, from which it is fed, via hoppers, to the firebox, where it is burned with little or no waste. Steam is raised in a boiler and used to power the ship's steam turbines.

Right *By using satellites for navigation, a ship's position can be easily and accurately located.*

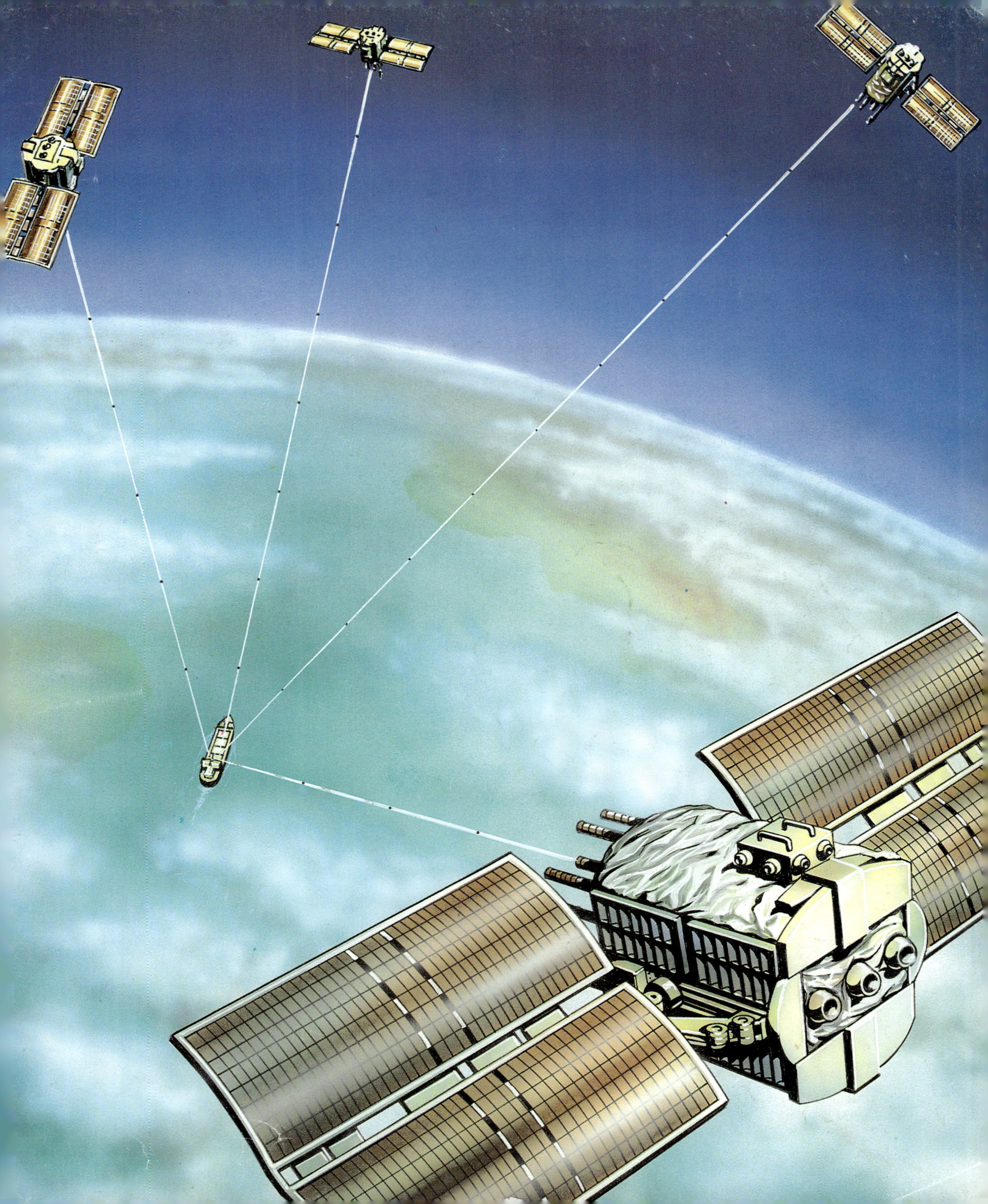

Surface transport ships are affected by the weather, but submarines remain unaffected by even the most violent storms. So some, at least, of the huge transport ships of the future may be submarines. Internal combustion engines need air and batteries, so these submarine transporters will have to be nuclear powered.

On the other hand, surface ships can take advantage of one of the world's most abundant forms of free energy – wind. Large sailing ships disappeared during the late 1800s, as coal- and oil-fired ships became more efficient. But as energy costs rise, sailing ships are beginning to reappear. The Japanese tanker *Shin-Aitoku-Maru*, launched in 1980, is a sail-assisted ship. Its rigid sails are set automatically by computer, and on a long journey they can save a large amount of fuel. Several other designs for sail-assisted ships have been proposed, and in the future sailing ships could once again become common on the high seas.

Vast submarine transporters will be nuclear-powered, but future surface ships may make use of sail power.

Aircraft of the future

Among the most spectacular of today's aircraft are the supersonic transports (SSTs) and the huge, wide-bodied 'jumbo' jets. These aircraft perform very different functions. Supersonic airliners transport passengers from one part of the world to another as quickly as possible. Wide-bodied jets, on the other hand, carry the maximum number of people as cheaply as possible.

The distinctively styled Concorde is the first supersonic passenger aircraft.

This research aircraft can pivot its wing to a 45 degree angle, which decreases drag and allows the aircraft to reach higher speeds.

Supersonic travel

The main problem with modern SSTs is that the cost of operating them is far too high. Concorde, the only SST so far put into service, has two major drawbacks – its operational cost and noise level. Future SSTs will have to be larger, quieter and more fuel-efficient. These aims will be difficult to achieve, but manufacturers do see a future role for supersonic airliners on routes used extensively by business travellers. They are currently experimenting with various ideas, including aircraft with titanium bodies and arrow-shaped wings. One promising engine for SSTs is the variable cycle engine. This can operate as a turbofan engine at low speeds and as a turbojet engine at high speeds. Turbofan engines are less noisy and more economical on fuel at low speeds.

In the future, we may see swing-wing SSTs. In one such design, both wings swing backwards for supersonic flight. In another, asymmetrical design, the wing can be 'pivoted' to various angles.

Jumbo jets and mammoth jets

Wide-bodied jets are likely to continue for many years in very much their present form. They will need to be quiet to comply with increasingly strict noise regulations and will therefore probably be equipped with turbofan engines. Alternatively, as fuel costs rise, new aircraft designs with propellers may appear. The fan of a turbofan engine is, in fact, a many-bladed propeller surrounded by a casing. A manufacturer in America has proposed doing away with the casing and reducing the number of blades to produce an eight-bladed propeller-fan.

Jumbo jets are designed to carry large numbers of passengers over long distances.

It is possible that wide-bodied jets could become even larger in the future, and mammoth jets may carry a thousand or more passengers. But such aircraft would need very long runways – up to several kilometres in length. So no existing airport could take mammoth jets.

Fuelling aircraft

Aviation fuel, like many other fuels, is derived from oil and is therefore becoming increasingly expensive. One possible new fuel could be synthetic kerosene made from coal, but the most promising fuel is liquid hydrogen.

One advantage of hydrogen is that, for a given energy output, it weighs one-third the weight of the equivalent amount of aviation kerosene. This means that take-off is much easier and more economical and, in the event of an emergency soon after take-off, little or no fuel has to be dumped so that the aircraft can land.

However, hydrogen does take up about four times the space of its energy-equivalent in kerosene. So fuel tanks of any future hydrogen-powered aircraft will have to be much larger. At present, hydrogen is expensive to manufacture, but in time it is hoped that methods will be devised for producing hydrogen using nuclear or solar energy. If hydrogen can be produced cheaply, then supersonic transport will become a much more economical proposition.

In future, we may see some aircraft with many-bladed propellers.

Megalifter airship
Hold for carrying enormous payloads
Russian three-hulled airship

Airships

The disastrous crashes of the R.101 and the *Hindenberg* in the 1930s prevented the development of airships for over forty years, except for a few built by Goodyear for publicity purposes. Recently, however, new airships made from safer modern materials have been developed. Instead of being filled with flammable hydrogen, they contain the inert gas helium. This was once rare and expensive, but is now found in old natural gas and oil fields, and is a by-product in the production of nuclear energy. Today there are a number of airships in use, such as the non-rigid airships and the larger, rigid-framed airships.

In future, we may travel in enormous mammoth jets, and spectacular airships like these may take to the skies.

A mammoth jet designed to carry hundreds of passengers

Airship Industries' Skyship 500 *preparing for take-off.*

Airships have the advantage of not needing runways, and are also more economical than aeroplanes or helicopters because they use very little power when taking off. They can also travel for much longer periods of time before needing refuelling. Surprisingly, perhaps, a modern airship can reach speeds of up to 220 km/h (137 mph) and can withstand anything from a tropical storm to a polar blizzard.

The future of airships is assured. At present, their uses include coastguard work, surveillance and cleaning up pollution, but their range of tasks is likely to increase. A Russian design for a three-hulled, nuclear-powered airship will be capable of carrying 300 tonnes of cargo or 1,600 passengers.

Other designs include airship variants that look like huge aeroplanes filled with helium. Such aircraft will have wingspans of over 160 metres (525 feet) and will be designed to fly at 300 km/h (187 mph) with enormous payloads. Perhaps a more feasible idea is an airship crane which would be capable of lifting over 50 tonnes.

Small aircraft

In addition to large transporters, there will always be a need for smaller aircraft. As now, there will be small, fast jets for business travellers and for military purposes. Helicopters will still have an important role, as will VTOL (vertical take-off and landing) and STOL (short take-off and landing) aircraft.

Flying for fun will also still be possible. Small, light solar-powered aircraft may become a common sight and hot-air ballooning is likely to become an increasingly popular pastime. Manufacturers are experimenting with new fabrics, such as Kevlar, and low-energy, solar-heated balloons which can remain in flight indefinitely.

Hot-air ballooning will continue to be a popular leisure activity.

Space transport

Future forms of Earth-based transport may not be all that different from those of today. They may be larger or sleeker and faster, but the basic types will be much the same. Space travel, on the other hand, may develop dramatically, bringing totally new forms of transport.

The Columbia *Space Shuttle returning to Earth after completing a mission in space.*

Intercontinental rockets

One new form of transport might work in the same way as a present-day ballistic missile. A rocket could be launched from a specific point on the Earth's surface at a precise angle and speed, so that it would land in the desired place. In this way, it might be possible to send transporter rockets very rapidly from one side of the world to the other. Goods could be sent in capsules similar to those used by the early astronauts. A capsule would be launched by rocket to travel outside Earth's atmosphere. Upon re-entry it would be protected by a heat shield and during the final stage of descent, the capsule could be slowed down by parachutes or retrorockets.

Passengers could also be transported using craft similar to present-day Space Shuttles – the ultimate form of high-speed travel.

A possible satellite solar power station with the Space Shuttle and a Heavy Lift Launch Vehicle (HLV).

Into space

The need for space travel in the future will depend largely on how plans for space stations, solar power stations and lunar bases develop. In twenty years or so, there could be many space stations orbiting the Earth. Some will specialize in repairing satellites, others will be the bases of construction sites, and yet others will be used purely for research. All these stations will require vast amounts of materials, which will have to be ferried up from Earth. And if solar power stations are ever built, it is estimated that over one million tonnes of material will have to be ferried up each year. To achieve this, huge, capsule-like space freighters or 'Heavy Lift Launch Vehicles' (HLLVs) will be used. Each day, ten of these spacecraft will be launched into space, where they will quickly unload their contents and return to Earth.

Once the major construction work is completed, spacecraft resembling today's Shuttle will be needed. One proposed successor to the Shuttle is known as Star-Raker, designed by Rockwell International. This huge aeroplane-like spacecraft will have a wingspan of 107 metres (351 feet) and ten turbofan engines. It will take off like an ordinary aeroplane, but at a height of about 14 kilometres (9 miles), three additional rockets will boost it into space to a maximum height of 480 kilometres (300 miles). There Orbital Transfer Vehicle (OTVs) will link up with the Star-Raker craft. The OTVs will carry satellites to their required orbits, boost spacecraft towards other planets and carry materials and people to space stations.

An artist's concept of the Star-Raker.

American space exploration is co-ordinated at Mission Control, Houston.

To the planets and the stars

The main problems with deep space travel is the time it takes to cover the huge distances to other planets and stars. This makes it impossible at present for man to undertake such journeys. Even the trip of one of our closest neighbours, the planet Mars, takes eleven months. So in the foreseeable future, journeys into deep space will be made only by unmanned robot probes.

Another problem of deep space travel is that ordinary rockets run out of fuel too quickly to be of any use over such vast distances. One proposed solution to this problem would be a starship powered by nuclear fusion. The starship, known as *Daedalus*, would be propelled by relatively small rockets to the planet Jupiter. There, it would process hydrogen fuel from the planet's atmosphere. Then, with its nuclear pulse motor producing a series of controlled nuclear explosions, the starship will leave the Solar System at high speed. It should reach Barnard's star (the second closest star to the Sun) in just under fifty years.

An ion-drive motor is another type of motor that could be used in spacecraft. It produces forward thrust by ejecting a stream of charged atomic particles, or ions, from its nozzles. For travel in the Solar System, the electrical energy needed to power the motor could be supplied by large arrays of solar cells. A nuclear reactor would supply the energy required for interstellar travel.

After 1,000 days in space, a spacecraft powered by an ion-drive motor could be travelling at over 360,000 km/h (225,000 mph). Even faster speeds are theoretically possible using a photon rocket, which would emit photons (light particles) from its 'exhaust' at the speed of light. But such an engine is at present technically impossible to build, and may always remain so. Even if future spaceships do reach such high speeds, it will still take many years to travel to other star systems. If people ever make such journeys, they may do so in huge colony ships. But those who reach the spaceship's destination will be several generations on from those who set out from Earth.

An artist's impression of a rendezvous between future spacecraft.

Left An artist's impression of the Voyager 2 *spacecraft encountering Uranus on 24 January 1986.*

Glossary

Articulated Consisting of two parts linked by a movable joint.

Atomic Concerned with atoms, the basic units of matter.

Ballistic Refers to an object which, when fired at an angle into the air, follows a curved path due to the pull of Earth's gravity.

Battery A device for storing electricity, consisting of two or more electrical cells which contain chemicals.

Catalyst A substance which speeds up a chemical reaction without itself taking part in that reaction.

Catalytic converter A device containing catalysts which convert pollutant chemicals in exhaust fumes into harmless substances.

Dry dock A large basin-shaped area for ships which can be pumped dry to allow work to be carried out on the ship's hull.

Electromagnet An iron or steel core wound round with a coil of wire. When an electric current is passed along the wire, the core becomes magnetised.

Electrons Negatively charged particles which surround the nucleus of an atom.

Generator A device which produces electricity by causing one or more coils of wire to rotate in a magnetic field.

Hydride Any compound of hydrogen with another element. Certain metals absorb hydrogen to form metal hydrides.

Inert gas A gas which is chemically unreactive.

Interstellar travel Travel from the planets of one star, such as the sun, to the planets of another.

Ion Either an atom that has had electrons removed, giving it a positive charge, or an atom that has had electrons added, giving it a negative charge.

Kevlar One of several super fibres called aramids that have been developed from nylon. It is five times stronger than steel.

Laser A device for producing a very concentrated, uniform beam of light.

Locomotive A self-propelled engine for drawing trains along railway tracks. This may be driven by steam, electricity or diesel power.

Microwaves A form of electromagnetic radiation, used in cooking and radar.

Momentum The continuous forward-thrust of an object resulting from its motion.

Nuclear reactor A device used to produce heat energy from the fission (splitting) of the nuclei of uranium atoms.

Pneumatic Concerned with air pressure.

Pollution The spoiling of the environment by harmful waste materials.

Retrorocket A small rocket engine attached to a larger rocket or spacecraft that produces backwards thrust to slow down the vehicle or make it move backwards.

Satellite A man-made device orbiting around the Earth.

Transmission The system of mechanical parts in motor vehicles which transmits the power of the engine to the driving wheels.

Turbofan A gas turbine engine in which a large fan driven by the turbine forces air rearwards, increasing the forward-thrust of an aircraft.

Turbojet A gas turbine in which the exhaust gases provide the thrust to drive an aircraft forwards.

UHF Abbreviation for Ultra High Frequency radio waves.

Vacuum A space containing no gas, liquid or solid.

Further reading

If you would like to find out more about transport, you may like to read the following books:

Transport on Earth by Neil Ardley (Franklin Watts, 1981)
Our Future in Space by Tim Furness (Wayland, 1985)
The World of Tomorrow by Robin Kerrod (Longman, 1980)
Aircraft 2000. The Future of Aerospace Industry by Bill Sweetman (Hamlyn, 1984)
Transport and Society series (Wayland, 1982)
Insight, a partwork magazine published by Marshall Cavendish (1980–82)

Index

Acknowledgements

The publishers would like to thank all those who provided pictures on the following pages: Air France 32; Mark Bergin 17; Courtesy of British Rail 18 (inset); Bruce Coleman Limited 19 (Orion Press); Compagnie du métro de Lille 25; Philip Corke 27, 29, 42; French Railways Limited *cover* (Lambert), 20–21 (SNCF); Lotus Cars Limited 11; Maltings Partnership 8–9, 30–31, 36–37; PHOTRI 2–3, 6, 7 (top), 15, 33, 35, 40, 41; Renault UK Ltd 10; Royal Society for the Prevention of Accidents 16; Science Photo Library 22 (Pacific Press Service), 23 (Martin Bond), 38 (Jerry Mason), 43 (P. Ryan), 44 (NASA), 45 (M. Paternostro); Swissair 34; Matthew Swoboda 39; Westinghouse Electric SA 7 (bottom); ZEFA 4 (Clive Sawyer), 5 (D. Cattani), 12 (Armstrong), 14 (Abril), 18 (Ballantyne), 24 (Justitz).